Wagner's World

María Lourdes Alonso

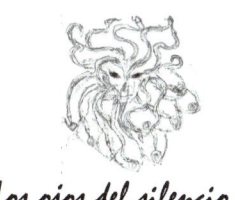

Los ojos del silencio

COPYRIGHT: Maria L. Alonso 2015

ISBN-13: 978-1514226742

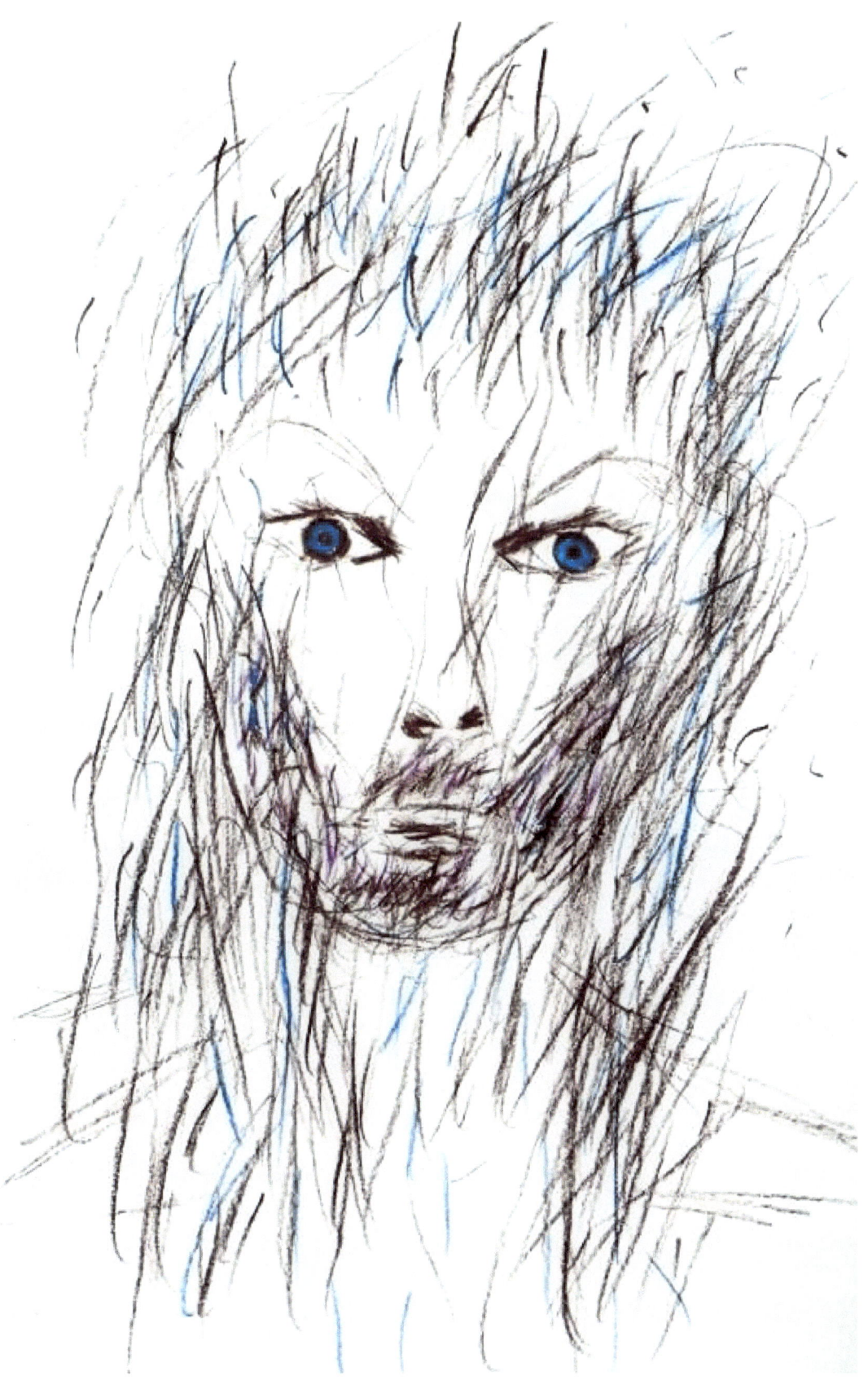

Der Fliegender Höllander

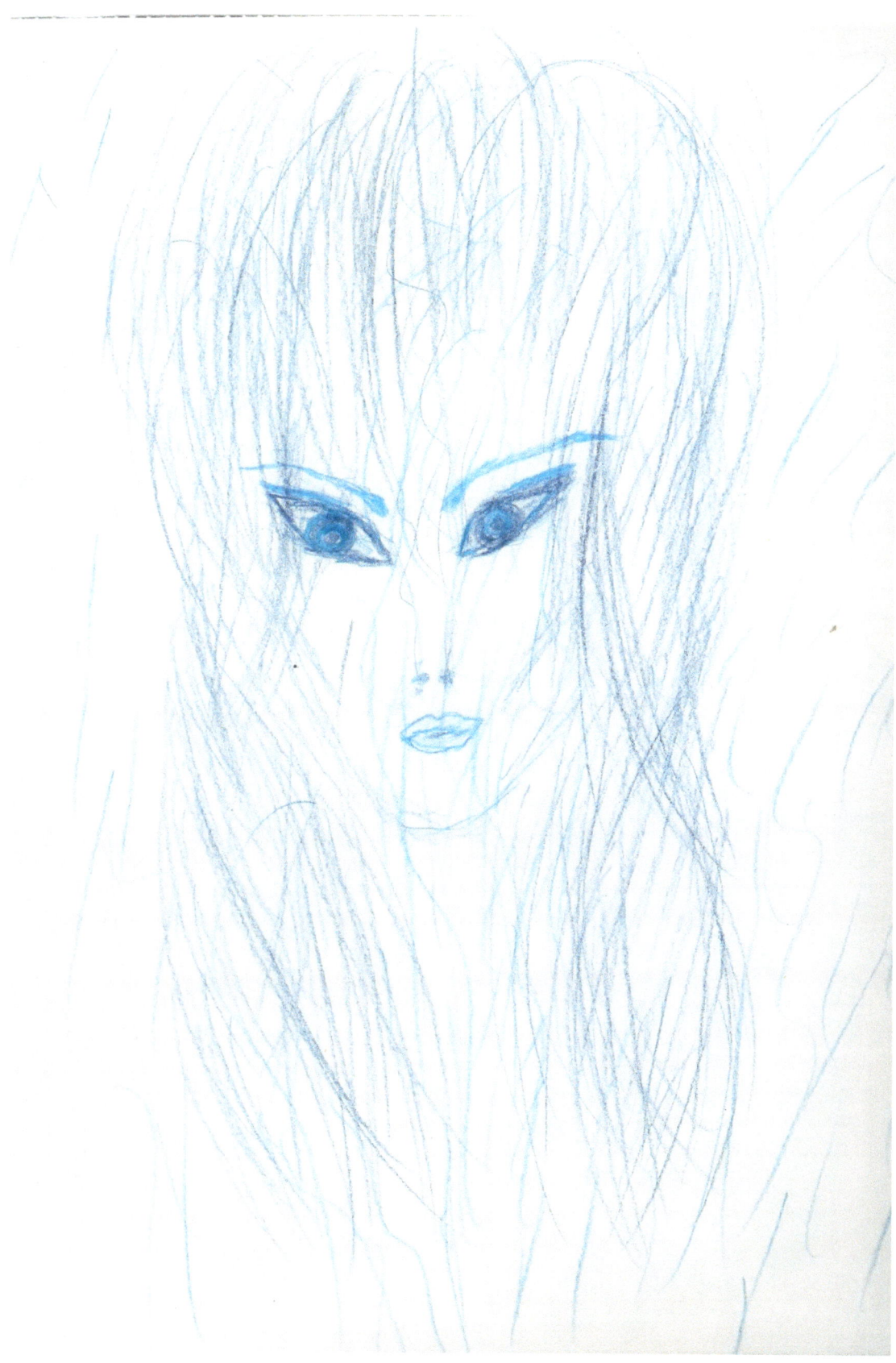

Senta

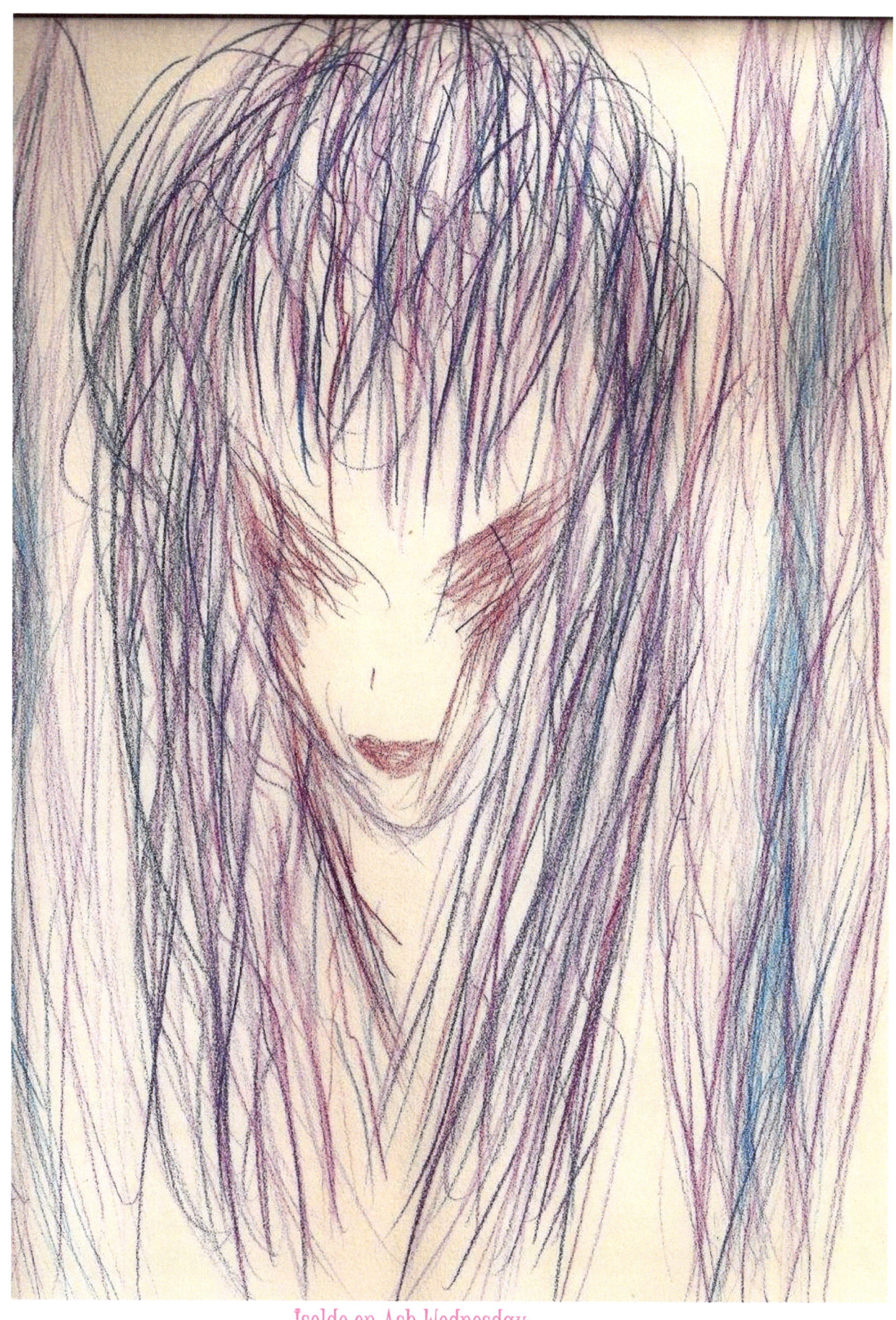

Isolde on Ash Wednesday

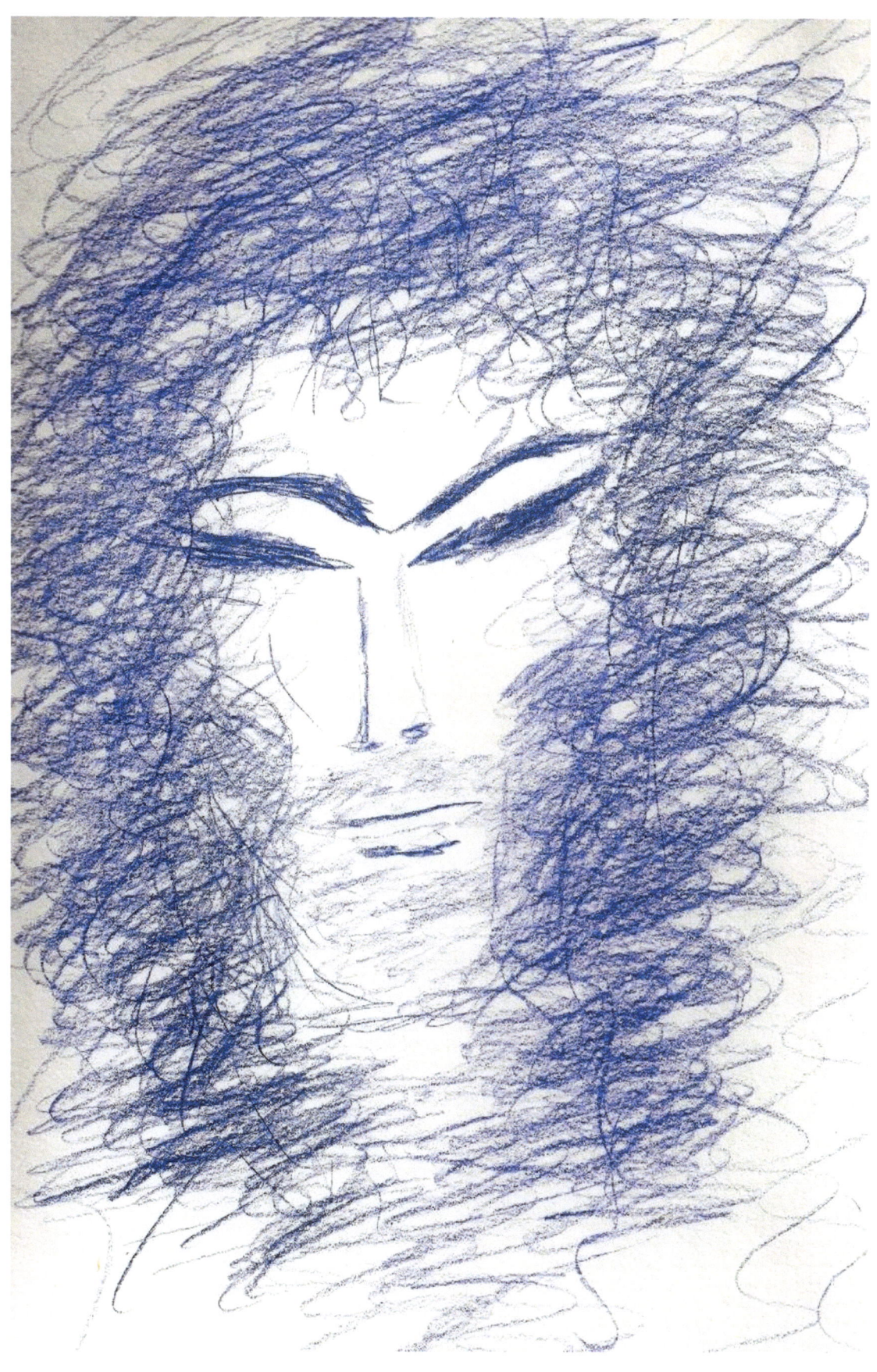

Tristan

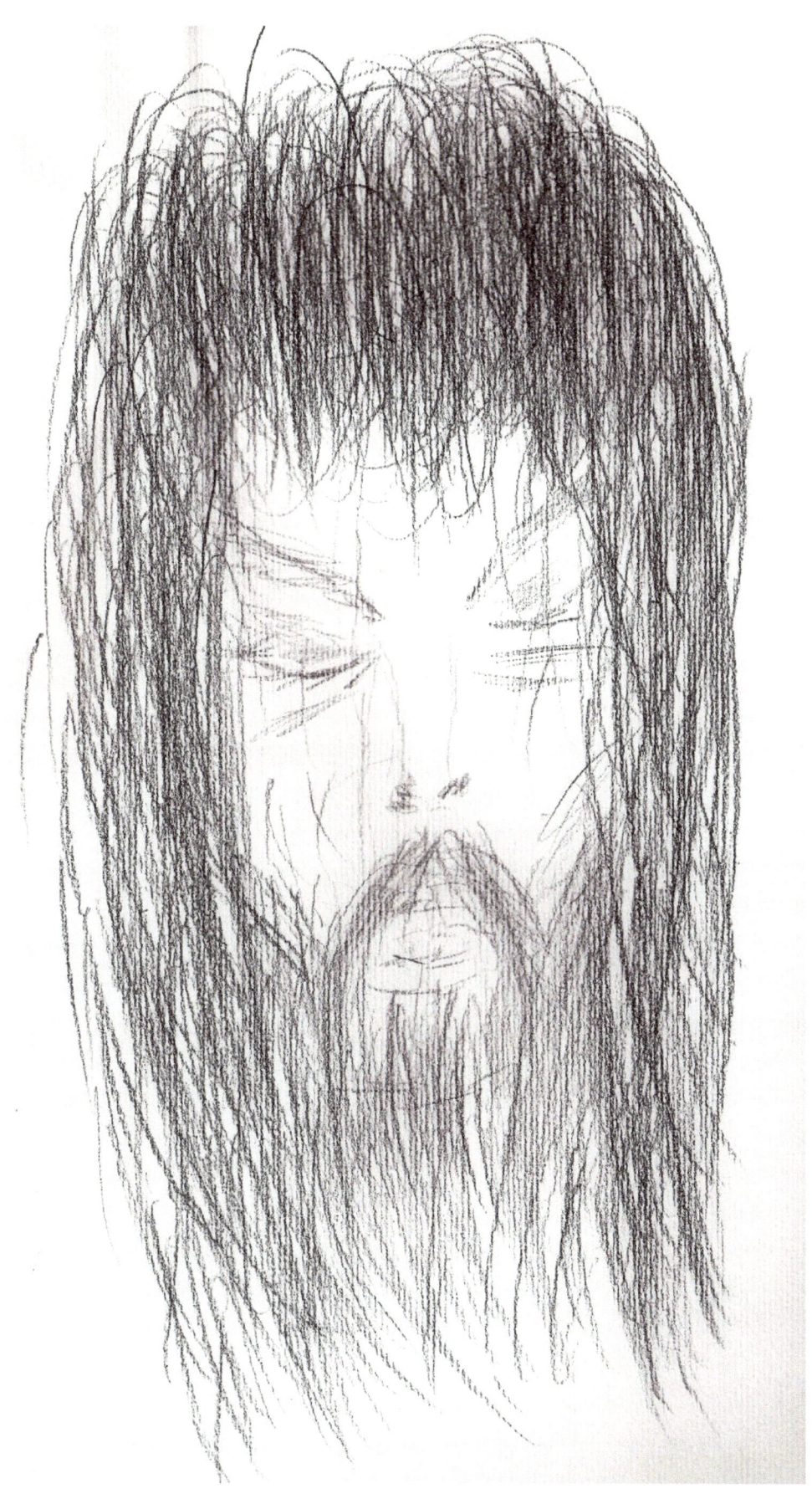

King Marke's Mourning

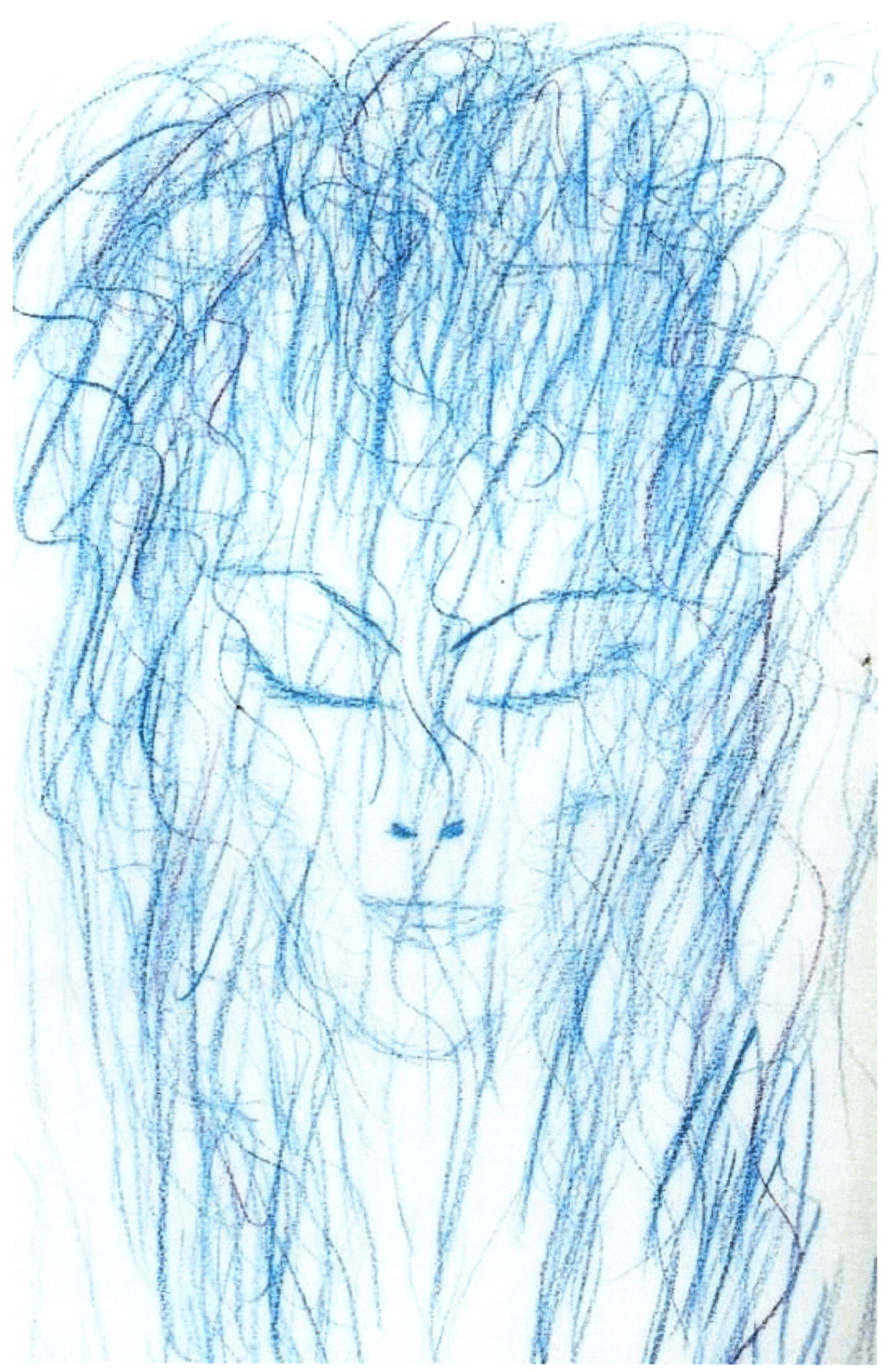

Brangäne

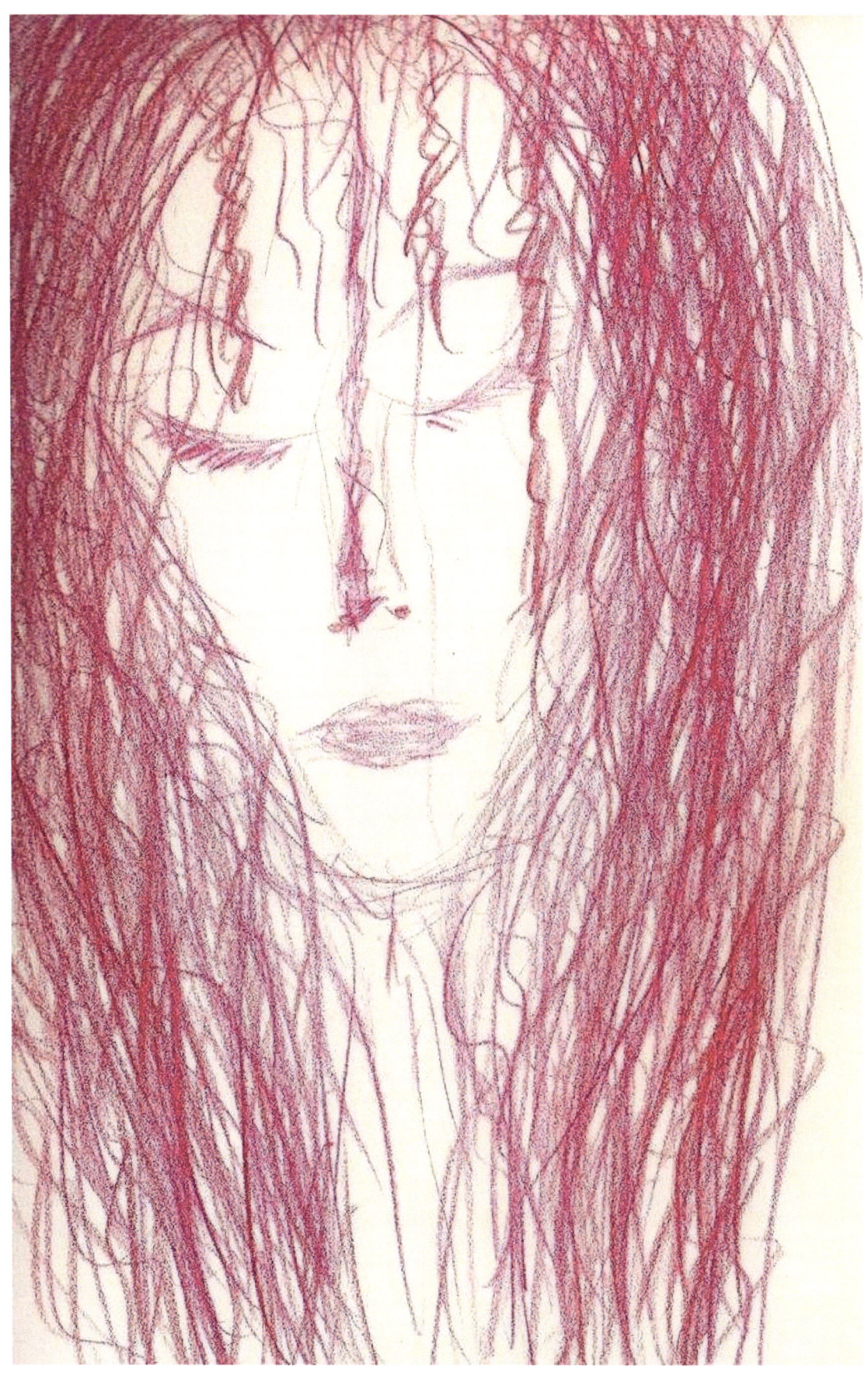

Isolde

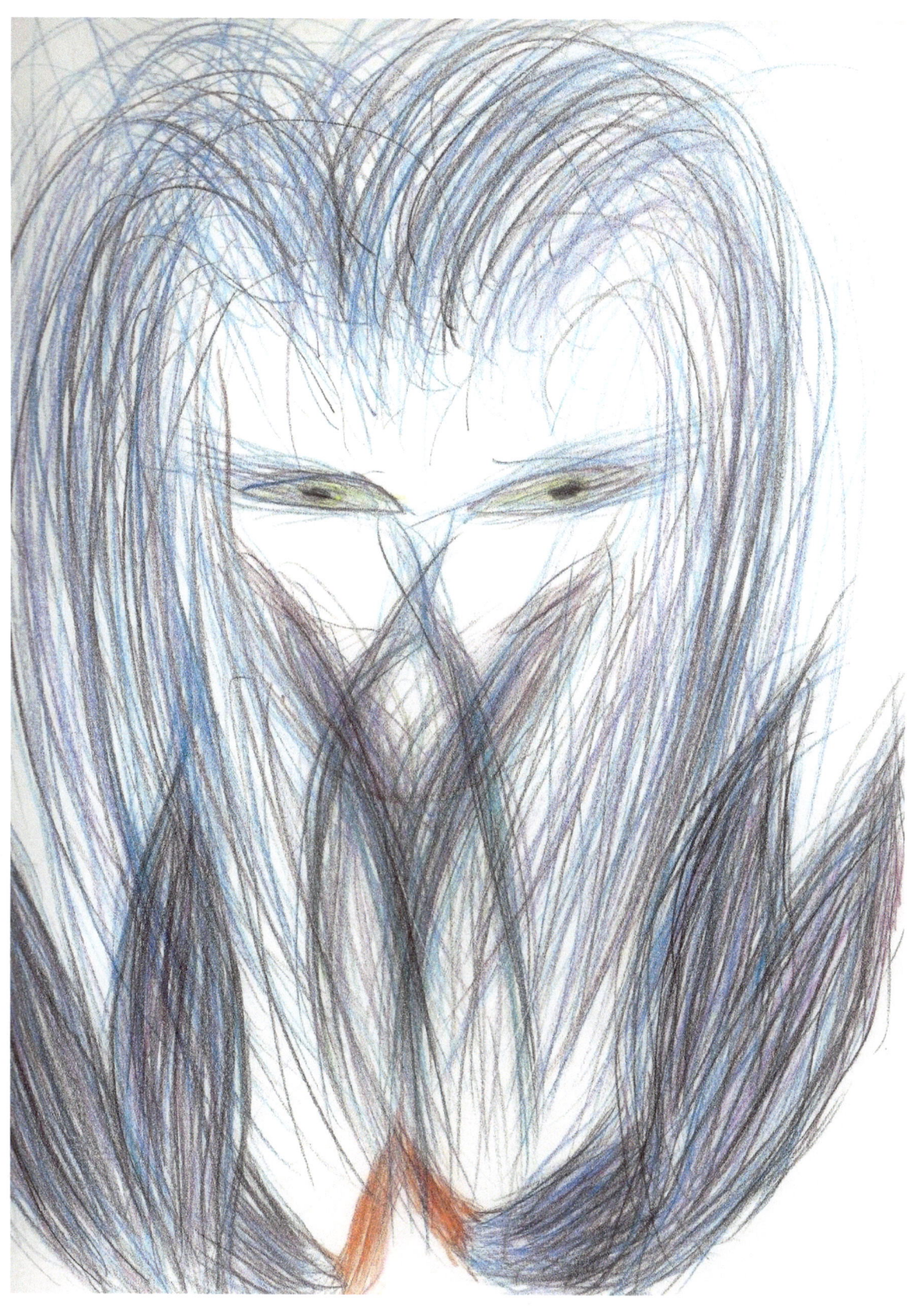

Wotan

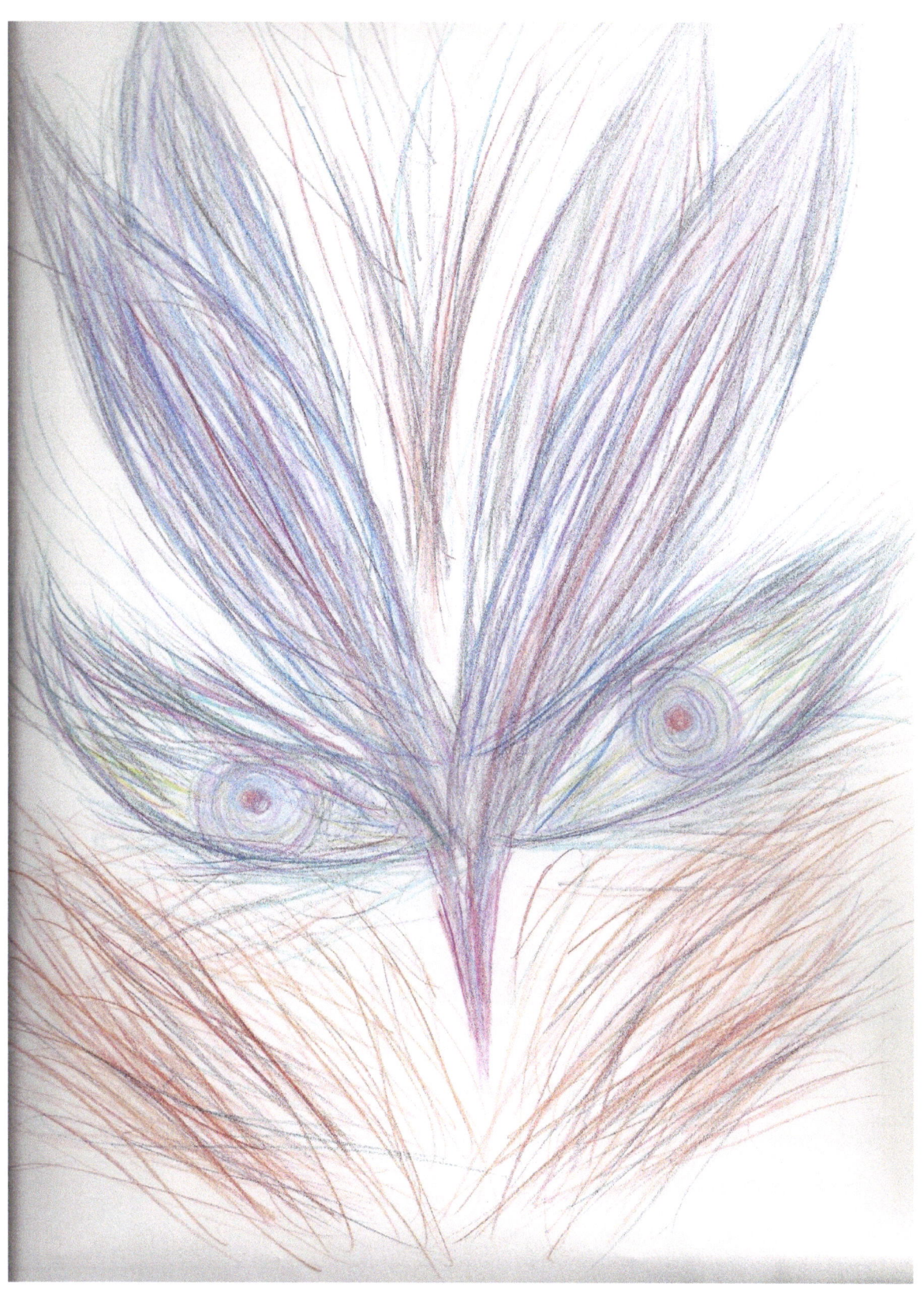

Wotan's look

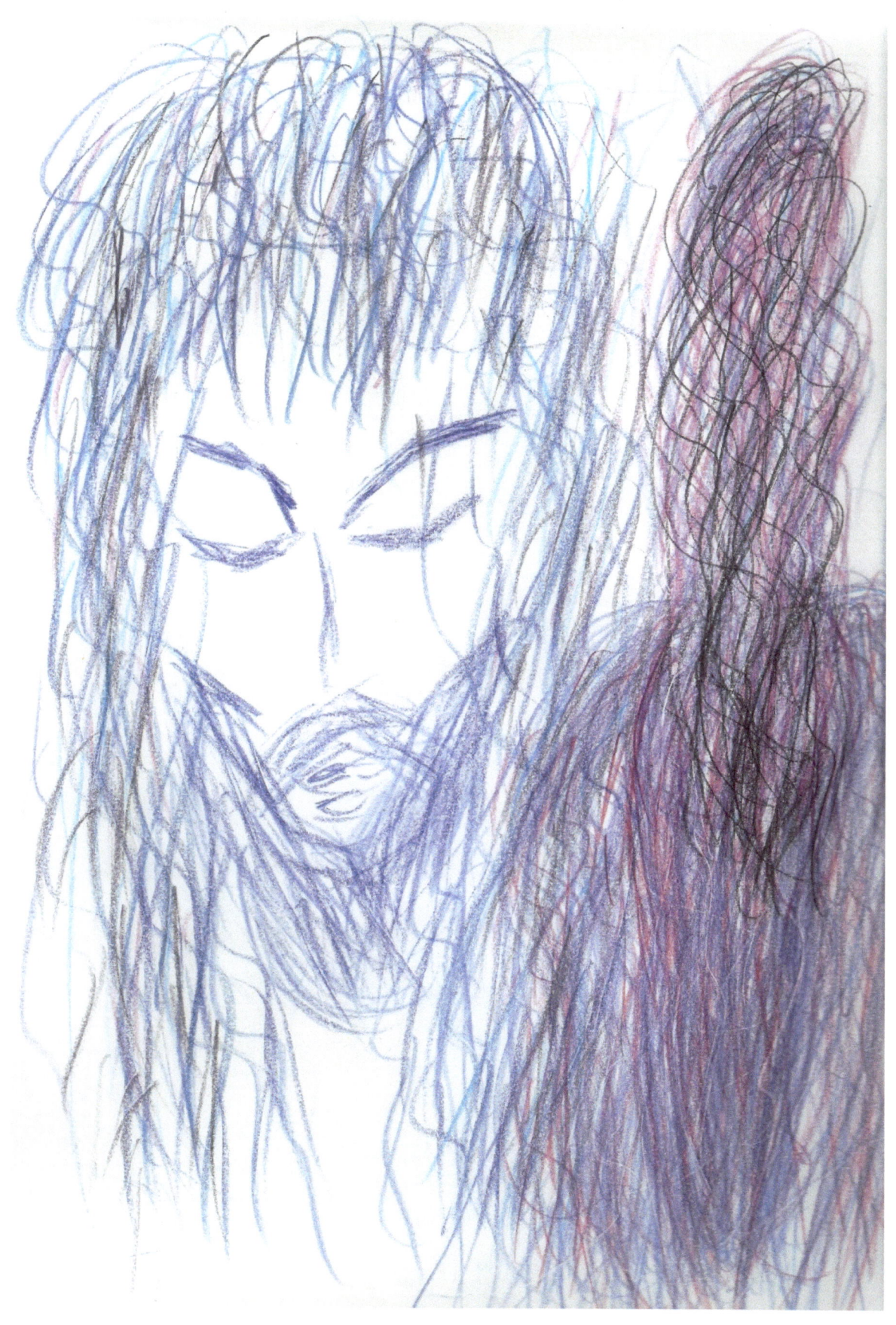

Siegmund & Sieglinde

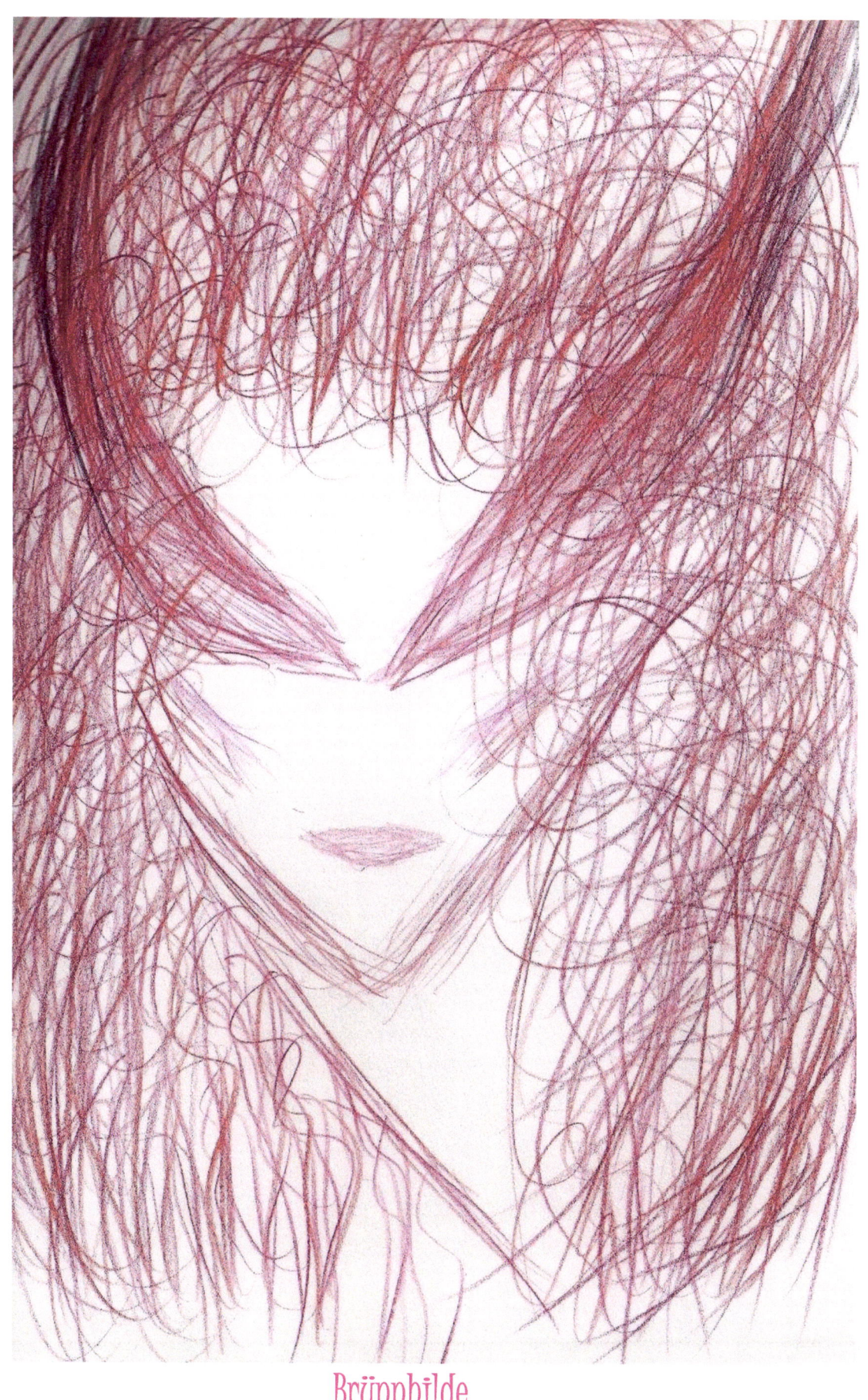

Brünnhilde

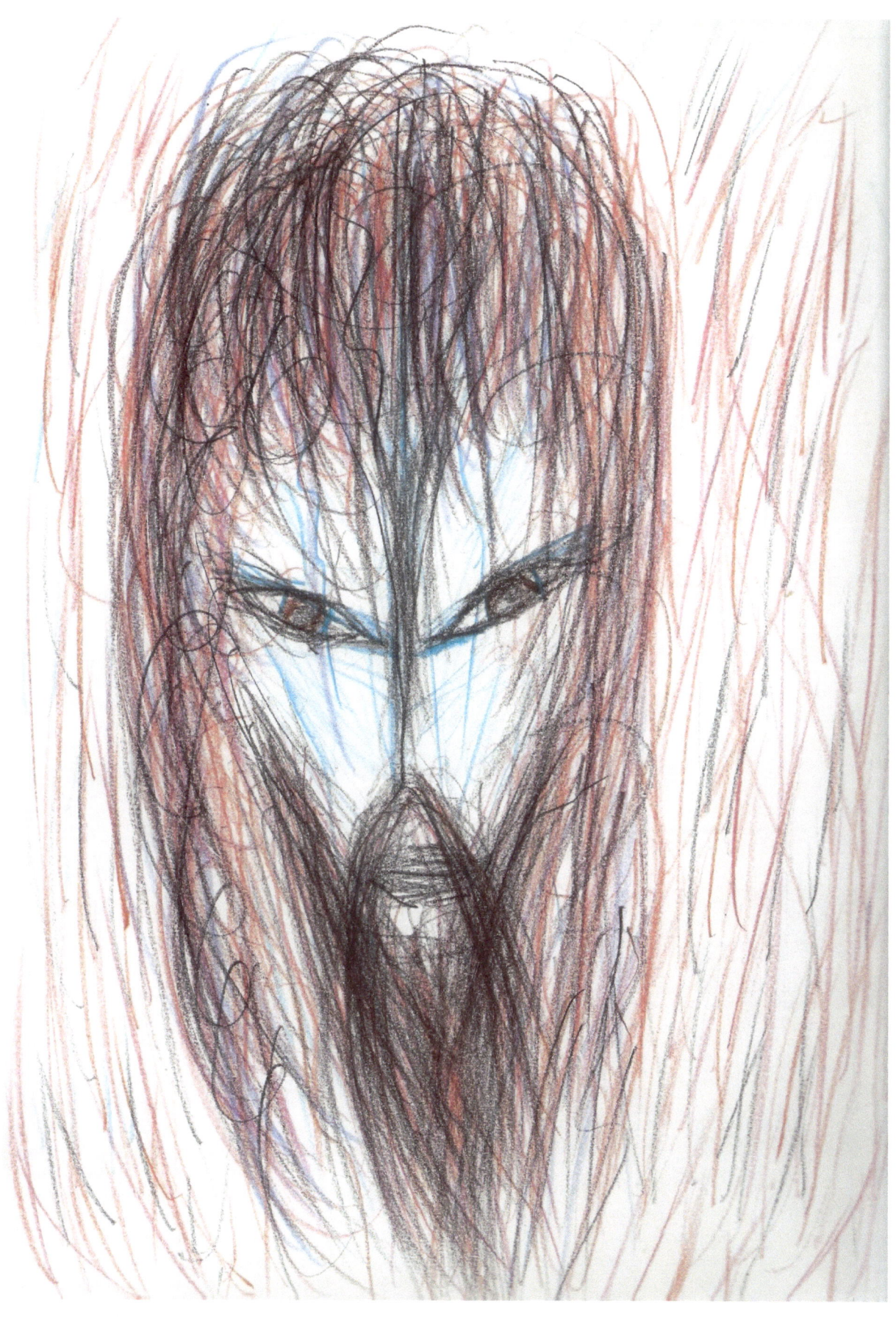

Wotan's Farewell

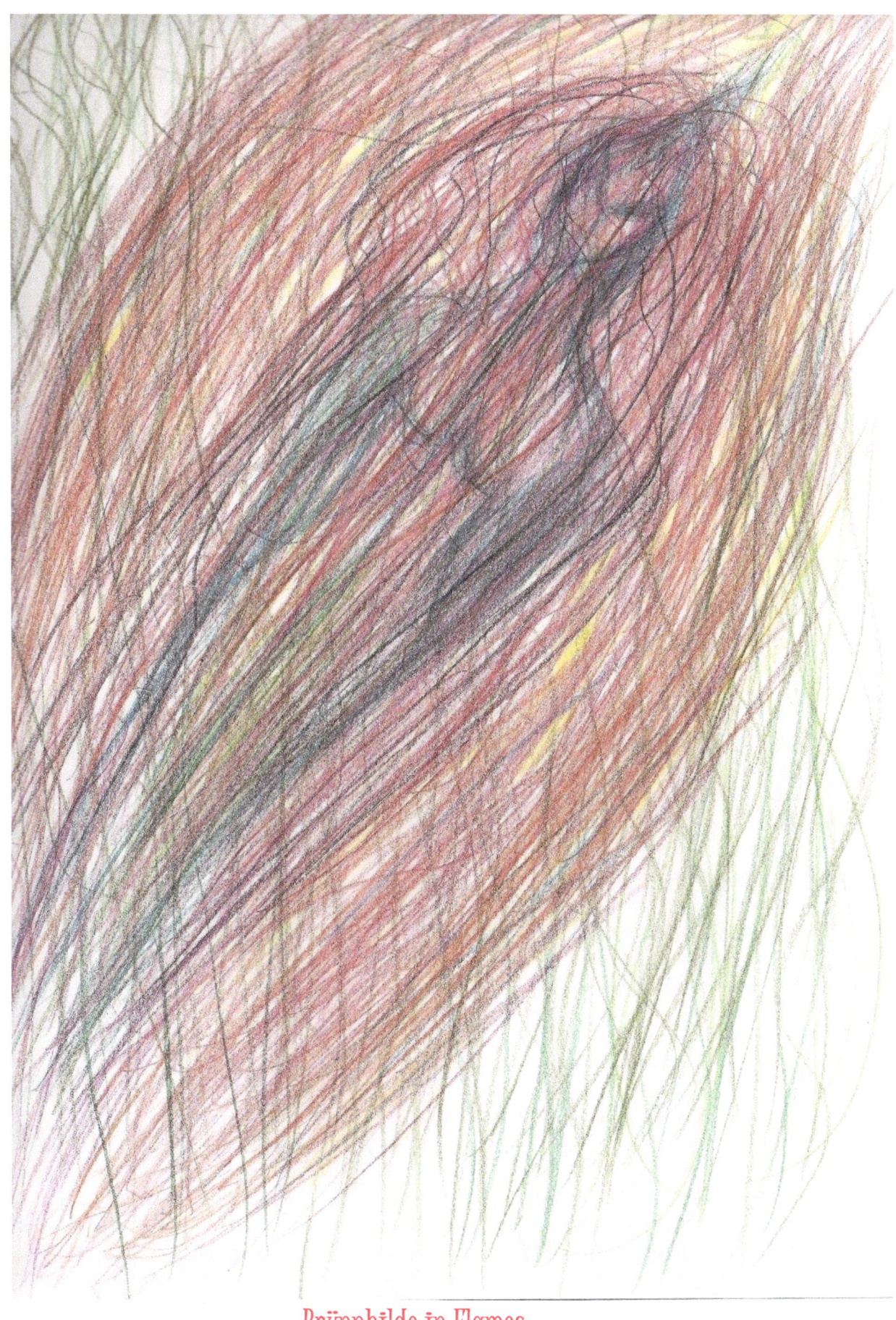

Brünnhilde in Flames

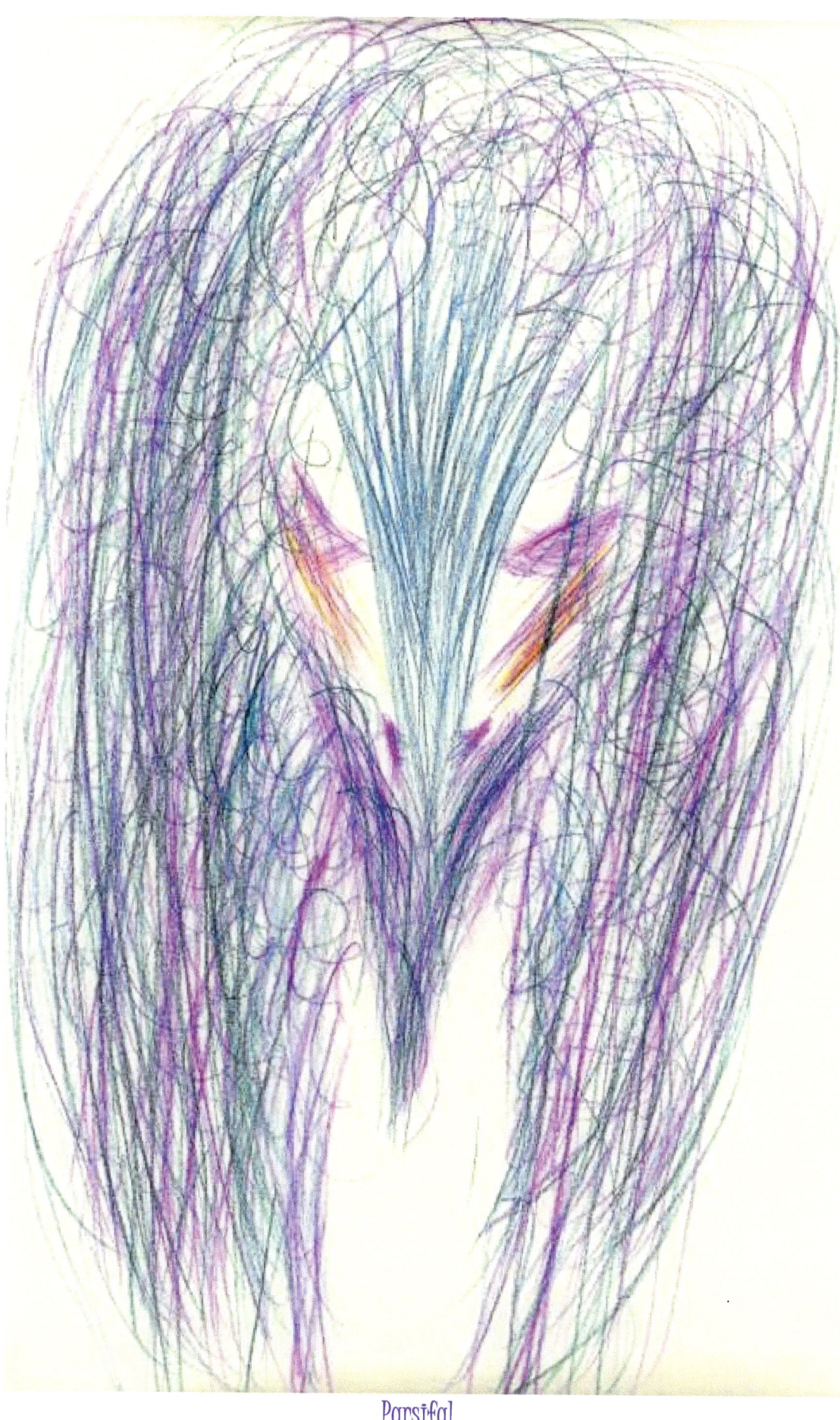

Parsifal

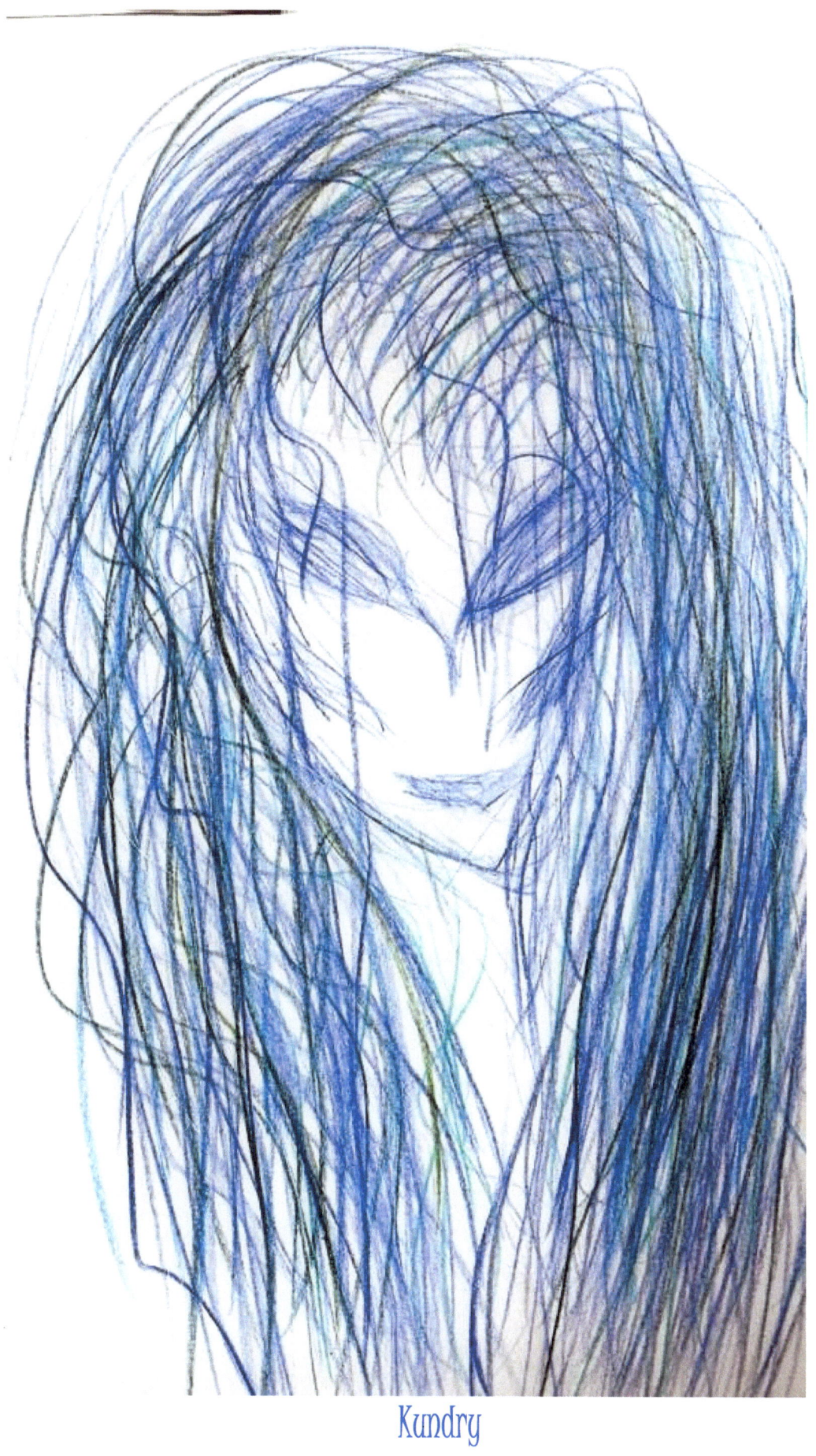

Kundry

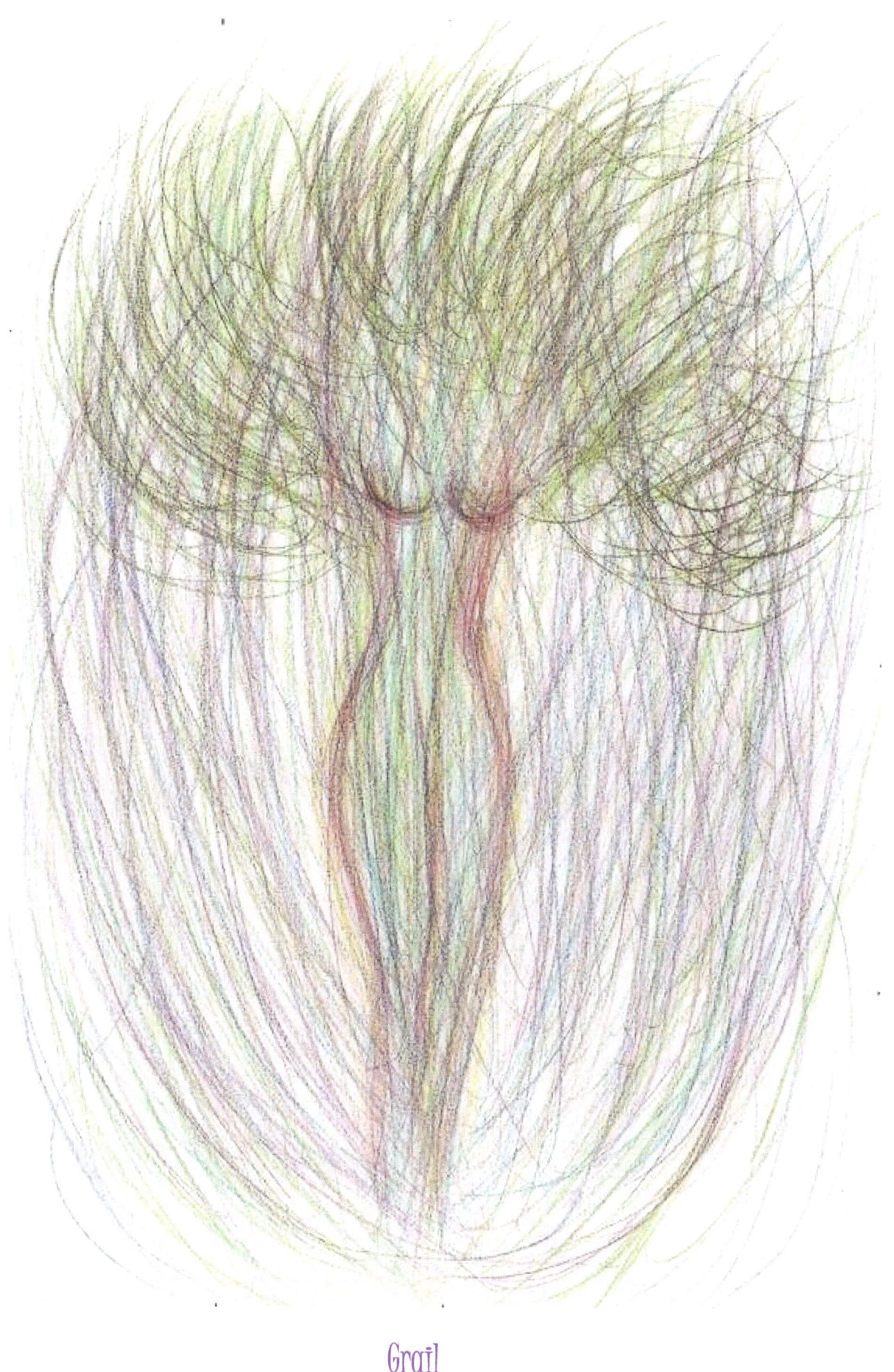

Grail

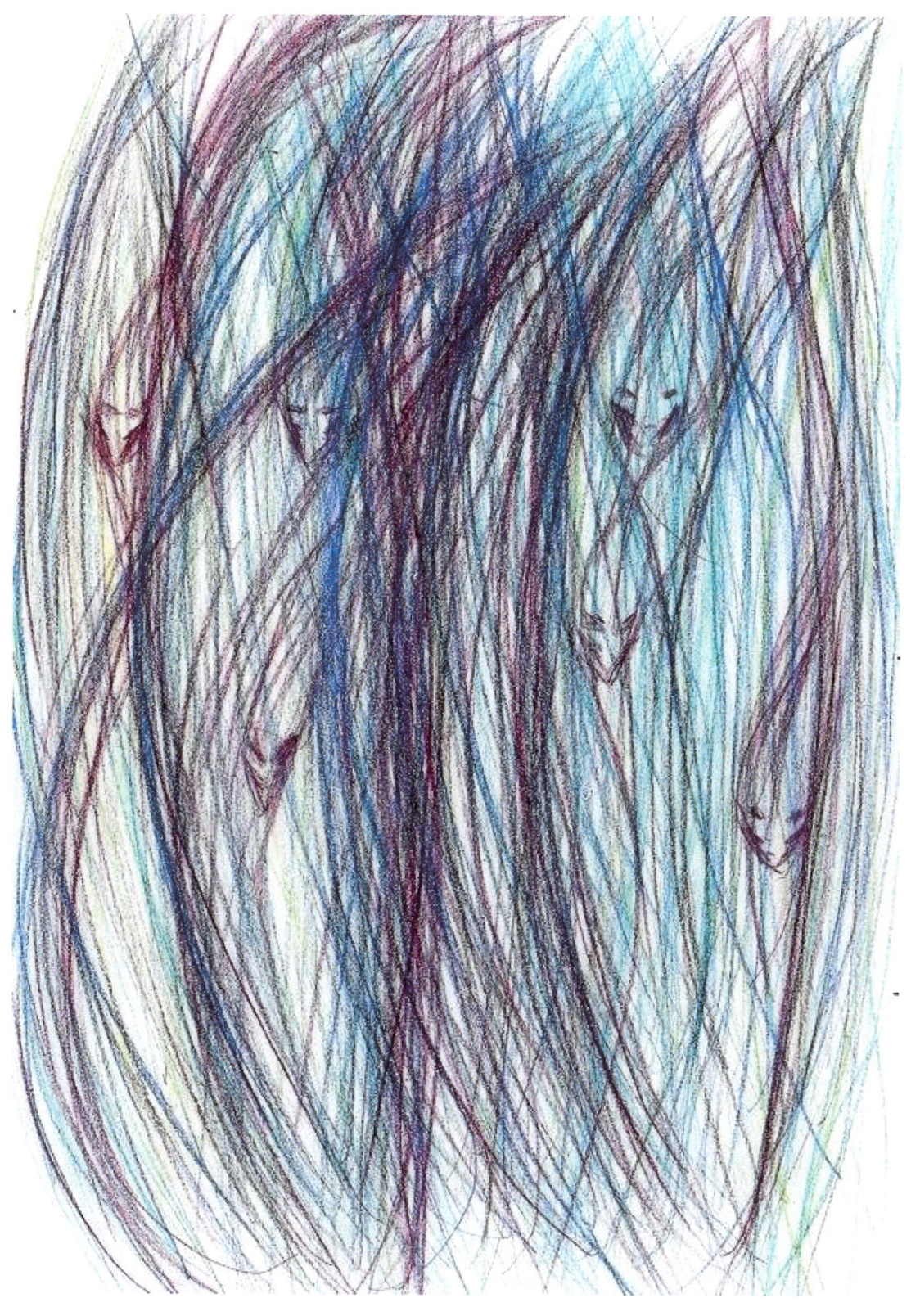

Monsalvat

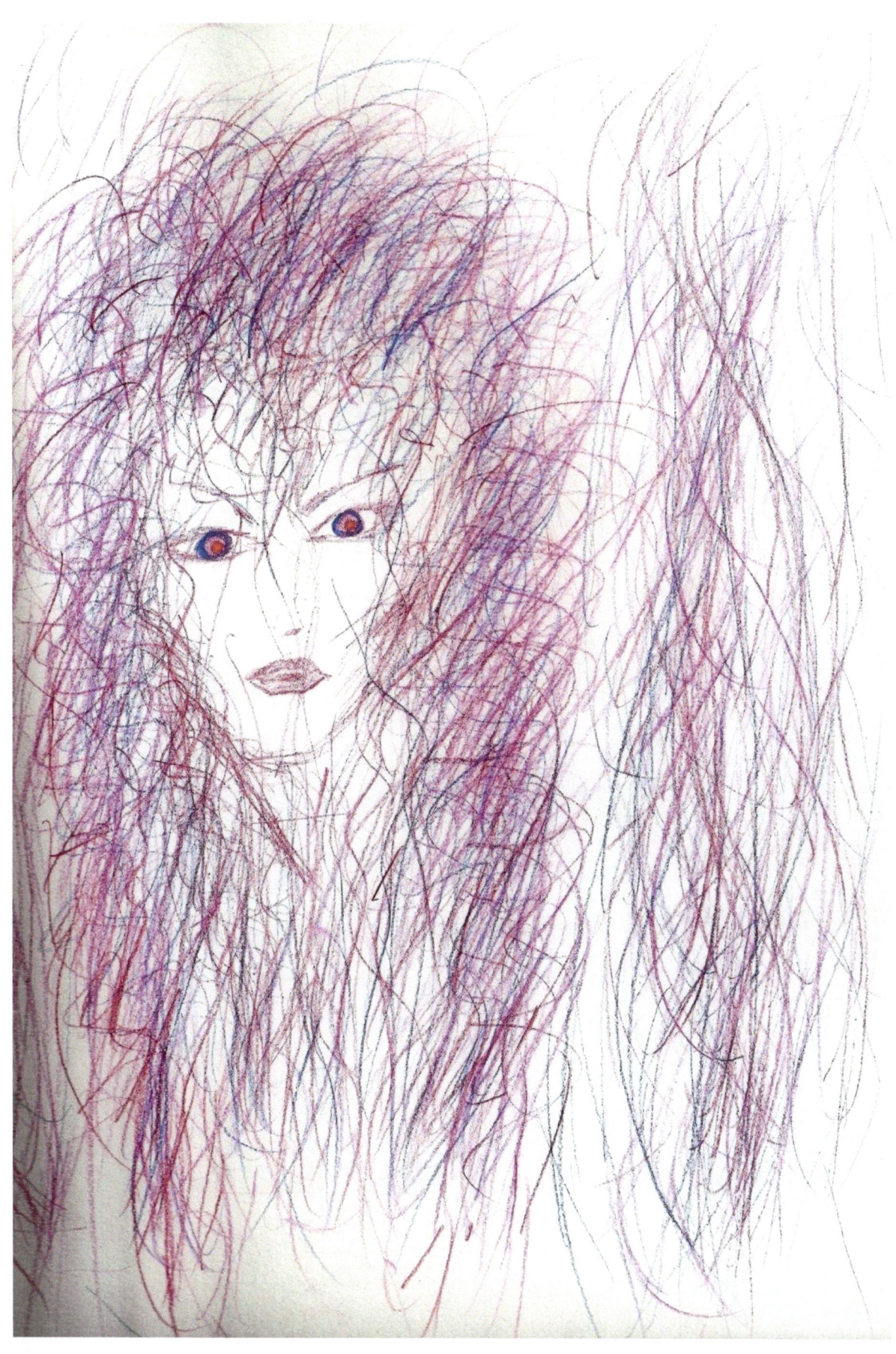

Kundry and Good Friday Spell

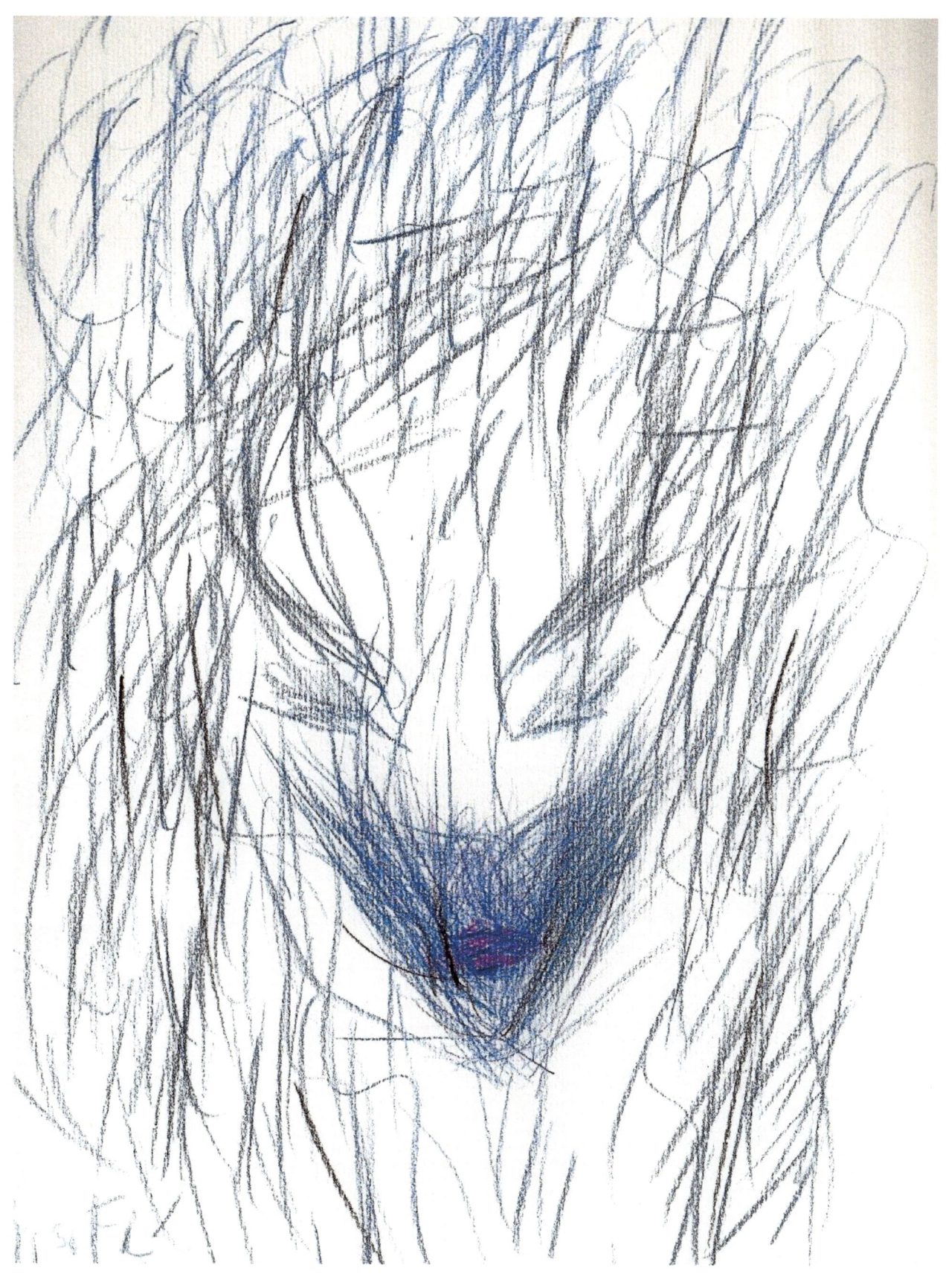

Parsifal. *Der Reine Tor*

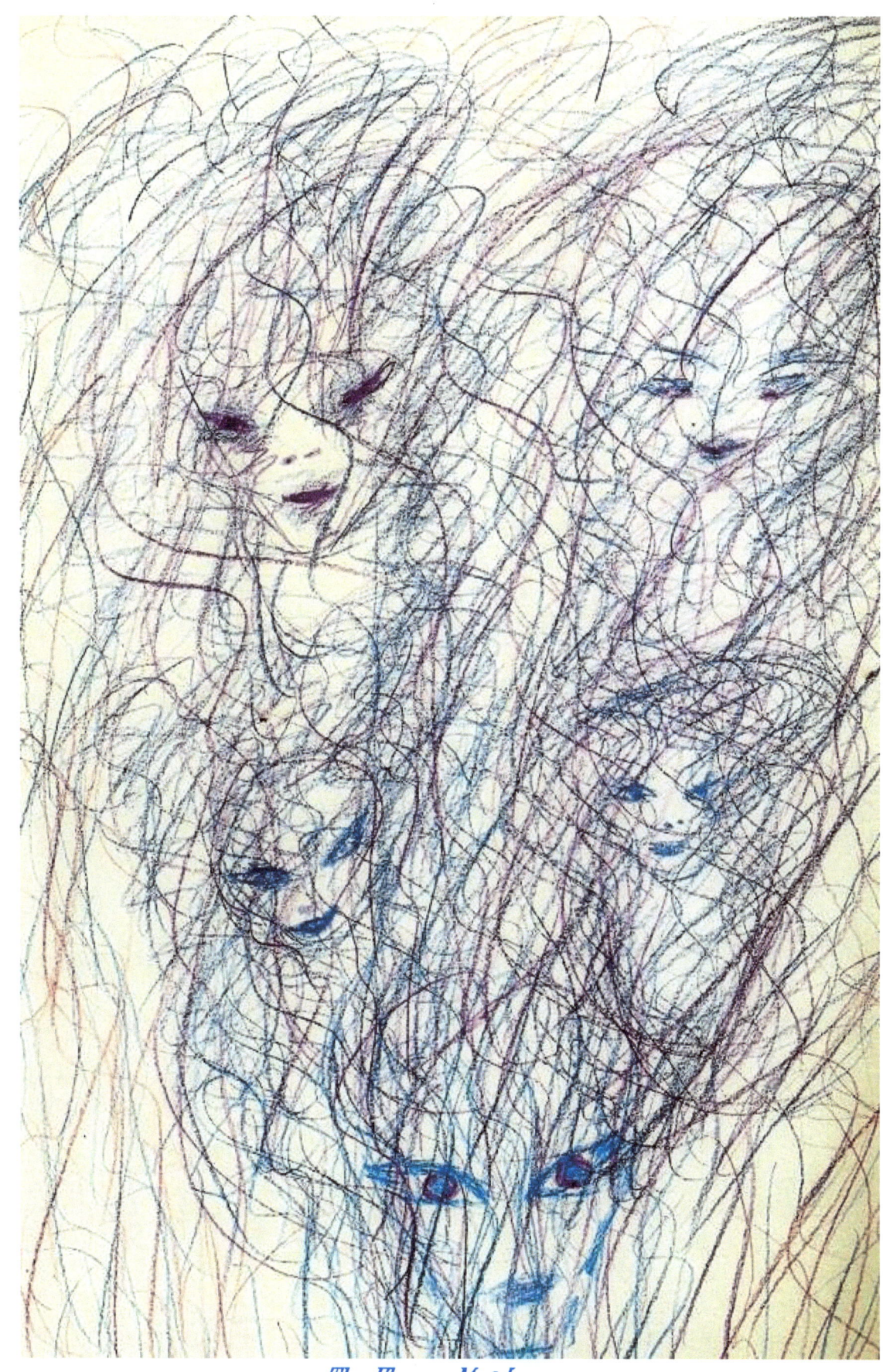

The Flower Maidens

INDEX